Feng Shui

Thorsons First Directions

Feng Shui

Simon Brown

Thorsons
An Imprint of HarperCollins*Publishers*
77–85 Fulham Palace Road
Hammersmith, London, W6 8JB

The Thorsons website address is:
www.thorsons.com

Published by Thorsons 2000

10 9 8 7 6 5 4 3 2 1

Text copyright © Simon Brown 2000
Copyright © Thorsons 2000

Simon Brown asserts the moral right to be identified as the author of this work.

Text derived from *Principles of Feng Shui*, published by Thorsons 1996

Editor: Nicky Vimpany
Design: Wheelhouse Creative
Photography by PhotoDisc Europe Ltd. except p76
Crystals picture, p76 © Tim Goffe

A catalogue record for this book is available from the British Library

ISBN 0 00 710337 9

Printed and bound in Hong Kong

Contents

Feng Shui

is an ancient Oriental system of organizing your home and workplace in a way that promotes health, happiness and success

Feng Shui is…

Feng Shui has been practised throughout China, Japan and Hong Kong over many centuries. Over time, different schools of Feng Shui have developed. There are four styles popular in the West. They are The Japanese Compass Method, The Eight Houses, The Flying Star School and the Form School. The Japanese Compass Method, The Eight Houses and The Flying Star School all use a compass as the basis for deciding how the energy in each part of a building will influence the occupants. The form school uses the shape of the landscape to orientate the Feng Shui energies. These different approaches are often combined. This book is based on the Japanese Compass system.

The Compass Method

This method uses a compass to determine the location of eight different areas, each of which experiences a particular type of energy. The features of the house, the function of rooms and the shape of the house are examined to determine their influence on the home according to the direction in which they lie. Nine Ki astrology is used to determine and understand the influence of the date and direction of the occupant's move to this building, and to establish the ideal time to implement changes to the building or the occupants' lives. The occupants' own Nine Ki charts will also influence the recommendations made for their home.

The Eight House Method

This system combines the position of the front of the building with its compass bearing to determine the nature of eight segments, known as houses, within the building. The occupants' own birth dates then determine the suitability of the whole house and of each of the eight houses within the building for the occupants.

The Flying Star Method

With this school the position of the front of the building, with its compass bearing, is used to orientate a chart onto which the building's own birth chart is superimposed. The features of the building and the surrounding landscape are then examined, and their effect on the building's birth chart calculated. In addition, at the beginning of each year, the Nine Ki chart of that year can also be superimposed over the building's chart to provide insights into possible problems that may arise in the coming year.

The Form School

With this method a compass is not used at all. The shapes and form of the surrounding area are represented by the classic phoenix, dragon, turtle and tiger, which then provide information on how energy flows through a building.

  This book concentrates on the Japanese Compass Method, along with a basic introduction to the Nine Ki astrology that goes with it.

The History of Feng Shui

There are many theories about when and how Feng Shui began. One of them involves the ancient civilizations that grew up along the banks of the River Lo in China. This area was plagued with destructive floods, which ruined the agriculture and buildings. Around 4000BC, a man named Fu Hsi made improvements to the river banks that prevented further flooding. He became emperor and the area began to prosper. The area that enjoyed the greatest success was located with the river to the east and protected from the north-east winds. Feng Shui literally translates as Wind Water.

One day, whilst meditating on the banks of the River Lo, Fu Hsi saw a turtle climb out of the water. To the Chinese the turtle is a symbol of life-long happiness and has great spiritual significance. Fu Hsi was amazed to notice a pattern of black and white dots on the turtle's shell. These dots were arranged in groups of between one and nine, and were laid out in such a way that whenever they were added together, whether vertically, horizontally or diagonally, they always added up to 15. Today, this is known as the magic square, and is fundamental to many forms of Feng Shui.

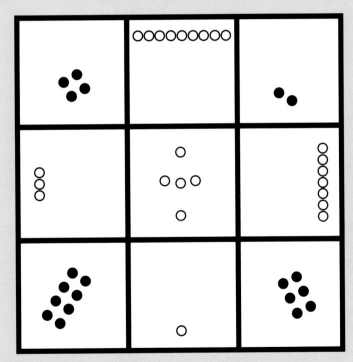

Pattern of black and white dots on the turtle's shell – The Magic Square

Finding a Consultant

At the moment there are no recognized qualifications or training courses for Feng Shui consultants. This means that you have to ask the right questions to find the Feng Shui practitioner that best suits your needs. Experience can vary from a few weekend courses to more than 40 years' work.

The following list will help you to find the best practitioner for your requirements.

1 Find out how they learnt Feng Shui. Due to the lack of Feng Shui courses, practitioners may have studied some form of oriental medicine such as acupuncture, shiatsu or Chinese herbal medicine. They will often be a member of their appropriate professional association. It is more common now for people with an interior

design background to become involved in Feng Shui. Find out how long they have been working as a Feng Shui practitioner and what type of clients they have worked with.

2 If you have a preference for a certain style of Feng Shui ask what type of Feng Shui they practise.

3 Find out what is included in the consultation. Are Nine Ki astrology, dates for implementing recommendations, or rituals to change the flow of energy included in your consultation?

4 Ask about fees. Some practitioners may be able to give you a fixed fee, others will charge by the hour. Be clear about what this includes. Does the fee cover a written report, travel time, travelling expenses and ongoing advice after the consultation?

5 Find out how long the practitioner intends to spend with you. Typical consultations range from one to two hours.

6 If you feel unsure, ask if you can contact his or her clients for references.

You will get the most out of a consultation if you trust and can communicate with the practitioner. If you make an appointment by telephone, always talk to the practitioner in person.

What to Expect from a Consultation

There is no standard Feng Shui consultation and each practitioner will have his or her own style. This varies from a visit and verbal advice, to a visit with a comprehensive written report. Some practitioners carry out rituals to change the flow of energy. It is also possible to have a consultation by post.

A typical Compass School practitioner might visit the building and meet the occupants. He will find out their dates of birth, when they moved to the building and where from. This enables him to make up their Nine Ki chart and calculate the direction in which they moved to this building. He might ask how their lives have changed since they moved to the building and find out what they want to achieve from their Feng Shui consultation.

He will measure the building and make floor plans, taking compass readings and marking them on the plans.

He may discuss the various options in terms of Feng Shui solutions to get an idea of what changes are realistic. If appropriate he may walk around the property and note any important features, paying attention to the neighbourhood, surrounding buildings and local landscape.

After the consultation he will draw out the plans and lay the grid of the eight directions over each floor of the building. He will check to see if there is any water close to the building. Then work on solutions and the best dates to implement them. A complete written report and drawings with solutions and dates to implement them should be sent to the clients. Most practitioners are happy to talk on the telephone if any further explanations, or help in implementing the recommendations is needed.

The Elements of Feng Shui

Chi energy

Oriental medicine and philosophy are based on the premise that along with all the physical aspects of our world there is a movement of a subtle flow of energy. In China this energy is called Chi.

Chi energy flows through our bodies in much the same way as blood, but while your blood carries oxygen and nutrients, Chi energy carries your thoughts, ideas, emotions and dreams. It is important to realize that your thoughts and emotions affect the quality of your Chi energy, and, as the Chi energy directly affects each of your cells, this can affect you physically. Equally, the quality of your cells influences the Chi energy flowing through them, and this in turn influences your thoughts. Typically, Chi energy extends 10 centimetres to 1 metre

outside your skin and mixes with the surrounding Chi energy. This makes your own Chi energy easy to influence.

Every building has its own unique movement of Chi, which determines the atmosphere of a place. Wherever you are, your own flow of Chi energy is constantly being influenced by your surroundings. Other people's Chi energy can also affect your own, along with the Chi energy of the surrounding land, and the type of Chi energy created by the weather. Feng Shui is primarily concerned with what we can do with in a building to help the occupants' Chi energy flow in a way that will bring better physical and emotional health.

From a much broader perspective, Chi energy flows not only throughout our planet, but through the solar system and galaxy. Our own planet generates a large movement of Chi. At the same time the surrounding planets radiate energy, which travels towards and into the Earth. Therefore, the Earth and surrounding planets have the ability to influence our own Chi energy. As the position of the Earth, sun and planets changes, so does the way in which Chi energy moves. Nine Ki astrology is the art of understanding these large-scale movements of Chi energy and predicting their effect on a particular person's energy.

Chi energy moves in the same way as wind and water. Visualize fast flowing water passing a sharp point. As it passes the point, the water

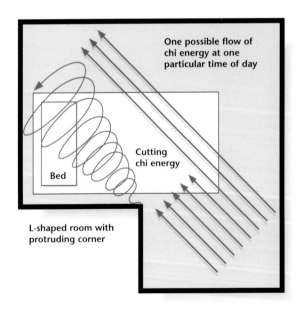

One possible flow of chi energy at one particular time of day

Cutting chi energy

Bed

L-shaped room with protruding corner

begins to swirl. The flow of Chi energy is exactly the same. It swirls around as it passes a protruding corner in a room. This swirling energy is called cutting Chi. Placing yourself within this swirling spiral of energy will tend to make your own energy swirl around, causing you to feel disorientated. If you were exposed over a period of time, for example if you were sleeping in front of such a corner, the constant immersion in swirling energy could eventually lead to ill health. Doors, windows, stairs, the shape of a building, the local landscape and the direction a building faces will all influence the way that Chi moves around your home.

Part of a Feng Shui practitioner's job is to identify how these features are affecting the flow of Chi within a building and find ways to create a more harmonious flow. Often, some areas of the home will be experiencing fast, turbulent energy, while others are stagnant. Feng Shui aims to create a situation where there is a harmonious flow throughout the home. By enhancing the flow of Chi energy in your own home, you can make positive changes to yourself, which in turn lead to a greater ability to realize your own dreams.

Yin and Yang

The *Yellow Emperor's Classic of Internal Medicine* tells us that by 2600BC the Chinese people already had great interest in the subjective effects of their environment. It describes how they had evolved the concept of a pair of interactive polarities present throughout nature, which they termed yin and yang. Nothing was seen to be absolutely yin or yang, but simply more yin or more yang when compared to something else. For example, resting is a more yin state than working, but more yang when compared to sleeping.

In the morning people are naturally more active and alert, a more yang characteristic than resting. In contrast, during the afternoon, people generally feel more mentally orientated, physically passive and sometimes even sleepy, which is a more yin characteristic. The classic definition of yin and yang is the shady and sunny side of the mountain, the sunny side being yang. Similarly, the sunny side of your home is considered to be more yang, whereas the shady side is more yin.

When the sun is up, the southern side of a home is constantly being refreshed by the sun's energy (in the northern hemisphere). People in this side of the home will benefit from this Chi energy. So if you want

to have more energy, to be active and inspired, place yourself in a part of your home that benefits from the sunlight. Here you will feel you can do more with less effort. The same principles can be applied to every aspect of our lives, from food to exercise.

The idea of balance is fundamental to yin and yang thinking. Everything naturally strives towards balance. However, to be more balanced may require unhealthy extremes of either yin or yang. For example, a long period of severe stress, which is more yang, might be balanced by a nervous breakdown, which is more yin. Lots of fruits, salads and drinks, which are more yin, will create a craving for salty, savoury foods, which are more yang. This constant flow can be seen throughout our natural environment. The day (yang) changes to night (yin). After we rest (yin) we go to work (yang).

People can also be more yin or yang. A more yin person tends to be relaxed, physically supple, sensitive, creative and imaginative. However, if this person is too yin they could become lethargic, slow and depressed. The opposite is true of someone more yang. A more yang person tends to be alert, quick, more physically active, able to concentrate and pay attention to detail. But if the person becomes too yang they would become tense, irritable, angry or physically stiff. Often a health problem can be attributed to an extreme of yin or yang. With a simple understanding of yin and yang one can easily tailor one's diet, exercise and lifestyle to one's own individual needs.

In terms of a house, buildings that have straight lines and sharp corners and are very angular are more yang than those that are more rounded, irregular and curved. You can make your home more yin by adding soft surfaces such as tapestries, big cushions and long curtains. In contrast, tiles, metal surfaces and glass create a more yang atmosphere. Colours also have a great influence. Bright, strong, stimulating colours make us feel more yang, whereas soft, relaxing colours make us more yin.

So, each person has more yin or yang characteristics and our environment has the ability to make us more yin or more yang. The idea is that if you can recognize whether you are too yin or too yang, you can then decide if you need to become more yin or more yang in order to feel more balanced. Once you know this, you can change your environment in a way that helps you.

The five elements

There are five different types of Chi energy, and each type is associated with one of the Chinese elements of fire, soil, metal, water or tree. Each element is further identified with one of five seasons of the year, the additional season being early autumn. To discover the characteristics of each type of Chi energy, think of the atmosphere at that time of year.

  For example, imagine looking at a tree as the sun rises on a spring day (tree). The overriding feeling is of energy moving up. Contrast this with watching a beautiful sunset reflecting off metal railway tracks in the autumn (metal). The feeling is of Chi moving inwards and becoming solid. Take yourself to the middle of a bright, hot, summer day (fire). Now the Chi energy feels as though it is expanding, radiating heat. Next jump to the opposite (water): a freezing, foggy mid-winter night. Everything is quiet and still. Finally, think of an early autumn afternoon. Imagine soil beneath your feet: heavy, solid and substantial. These are the qualities associated with soil Chi.

  The quality of Chi energy in your home will vary through the day as the sun moves through different phases. In the morning the part of your home facing east, where the sun rises, will soak up the upward

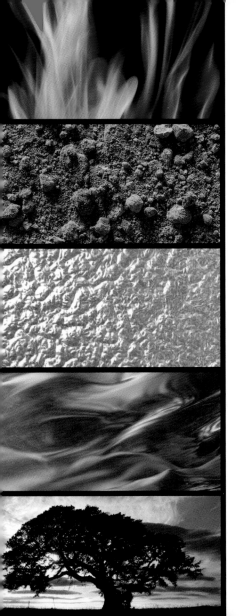

Chi energy (tree). As the day progresses, the sun will move to the south and charge up the southern part of your home with fire Chi energy, and so on until finally, during the night, the north benefits from water Chi energy. Soil Chi energy is associated with the centre of your home.

Think about your home and how each room is affected by the movement of the sun. This will help you decide which activities are best suited to which parts of your home. Generally, the east is ideal for activities that require more 'up' energy. The south, fire energy, is better for parties and social events. The more settled energy of the south-west and centre makes this a better place for practical projects. The west of your home is a romantic place to relax and conclude your day. The north, being winter and night, is an obvious place to sleep.

The five elements are strongly related to each other in the cycles represented in the diagram on page 22. The circle around the outside represents what is often referred to as the support cycle, whereas the lines inside the cycle depict the destructive cycle. So fire supports soil, which supports metal which in turn supports water, which supports tree. Tree supports fire, and so we return to the beginning of the cycle. If, however, the cycle is broken and one of the elements is missing, the influence of the preceding energy becomes destructive. Hence fire can have a destructive effect on metal, metal can have a destructive effect on tree, tree can have a destructive effect on soil, soil can have a destructive effect on water, and water can have a destructive effect on fire.

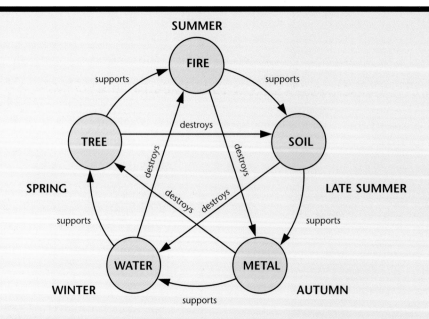

In Feng Shui both the supportive and destructive cycles can be used to help balance energy. Actual water, fire or metal are used to encourage changes in the movement of Chi energy. For example, it is considered auspicious to have water to the east of your home. This places water in a direction that relates to the tree element. The water Chi energy supports tree Chi energy. Therefore water to the east will enhance the energy found in the east. The support cycle can also be used to calm Chi energy. If there is too much Chi in the south-west, which is associated with soil, placing something made of metal in this location will absorb some of the soil Chi energy, as soil supports metal.

The Magic Square

Chinese Nine Ki astrology is used in Feng Shui to describe how energy moves at different times. To do this it uses the Magic Square first discovered by Fu Hsi in 4000BC. In Nine Ki astrolgy, each year is represented by one of the number charts shown opposite.

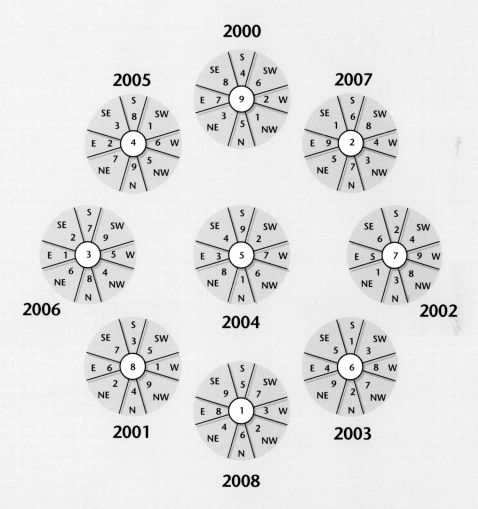

2000

2005

2007

2006

2004

2002

2001

2008

2003

The chart in the middle is called the standard chart. This is the chart where the numbers always add up to 15, whether you add them vertically, horizontally or diagonally. This standard chart always has the number 5 at its centre. Surrounding the standard chart are eight different charts. Each chart is referred to by its central number. So the standard chart is called the chart of five. The chart with 9 in the middle will be called the chart of nine and so on. Each year has its own Nine Ki number, which is the one that takes up the central position in the chart for that particular year, for example, 2001 is an 8 year.

Your Nine Ki Year Number

The year you were born with the date and time the year begins	9	8	7	6	5	4	3	2	1
	1901	1902	1903	1904	1905	1906	1907	1908	1909
	4-Feb	5-Feb	5-Feb	5-Feb	4-Feb	5-Feb	5-Feb	5-Feb	4-Feb
	19:03	0:57	6:55	12:40	18:36	0:28	6:13	12:09	17:53
	1910	1911	1912	1913	1914	1915	1916	1917	1918
	4-Feb	5-Feb	5-Feb	4-Feb	4-Feb	5-Feb	5-Feb	4-Feb	4-Feb
	23:41	5:33	11:11	17:01	22:53	4:34	10:31	16:18	22:06
	1919	1920	1921	1922	1923	1924	1925	1926	1927
	5-Feb	5-Feb	4-Feb	4-Feb	5-Feb	5-Feb	4-Feb	4-Feb	5-Feb
	4:00	9:43	15:34	21:28	3:13	9:06	14:58	20:49	2:46
	1928	1929	1930	1931	1932	1933	1934	1935	1936
	5-Feb	4-Feb	4-Feb	5-Feb	5-Feb	4-Feb	4-Feb	5-Feb	5-Feb
	8:31	14:19	20:11	1:53	7:42	13:28	19:13	1:03	6:47
	1937	1938	1939	1940	1941	1942	1943	1944	1945
	4-Feb	4-Feb	5-Feb	5-Feb	4-Feb	4-Feb	4-Feb	5-Feb	4-Feb
	12:36	18:32	0:20	6:15	12:07	17:57	23:51	5:39	11:26
	1946	1947	1948	1949	1950	1951	1952	1953	1954
	4-Feb	4-Feb	5-Feb	4-Feb	4-Feb	4-Feb	5-Feb	4-Feb	4-Feb
	17:18	23:03	4:50	10:40	16:29	22:29	4:07	9:52	15:42
	1955	1956	1957	1958	1959	1960	1961	1962	1963
	4-Feb	5-Feb	4-Feb	4-Feb	4-Feb	5-Feb	4-Feb	4-Feb	4-Feb
	21:29	3:15	9:07	14:57	20:47	2:38	8:29	14:24	20:17

Your Nine Ki Year Number

9	8	7	6	5	4	3	2	1
1964 5-Feb 2:28	1965 4-Feb 7:57	1966 4-Feb 13:46	1967 4-Feb 19:32	1968 5-Feb 1:19	1969 4-Feb 7:04	1970 4-Feb 12:50	1971 4-Feb 18:37	1972 5-Feb 0:23
1973 4-Feb 6:13	1974 4-Feb 12:08	1975 4-Feb 17:56	1976 4-Feb 23:48	1977 4-Feb 5:38	1978 4-Feb 11:28	1979 4-Feb 17:21	1980 4-Feb 23:10	1981 4-Feb 4:59
1982 4-Feb 10:53	1983 4-Feb 16:38	1984 4-Feb 22:27	1985 4-Feb 4:18	1986 4-Feb 10:05	1987 4-Feb 15:57	1988 4-Feb 21:42	1989 4-Feb 5:28	1990 4-Feb 9:20
1991 4-Feb 15:04	1992 4-Feb 20:51	1993 4-Feb 2:42	1994 4-Feb 8:27	1995 4-Feb 14:18	1996 4-Feb 20:10	1997 4-Feb 2:00	1998 4-Feb 8:01	1999 4-Feb 13:51
2000 4-Feb 19:39	2001 4-Feb 1:35	2002 4-Feb 7:20	2003 4-Feb 13:08	2004 4-Feb 18:57	2005 4-Feb 0:38	2006 4-Feb 6:31	2007 4-Feb 12:16	2008 4-Feb 17:59
2009 3-Feb 23:55	2010 4-Feb 5:40	2011 4-Feb 11:31	2012 4-Feb 17:28	2013 3-Feb 23:05	2014 4-Feb 5:05	2015 4-Feb 10:55	2016 4-Feb 16:40	2017 3-Feb 22:37

The year you were born with the date and time the year begins

The chart on pages 27–8 shows the Nine Ki year number for each of the years from 1901 to 2017. From this you can work out which number was in the centre of the chart in the year you were born. This is called your Nine Ki year number. Note that the Nine Ki year does not start on 1 January. Usually it is 3, 4 or 5 February. So a person born right at the beginning of the year will actually base their Nine Ki year number on the preceding year. For example, if you were born on 1 February 1962, you would actually use the chart for 1961. The times are given in Greenwich Mean Time. If you are born close to the time at which the year changes you may need to convert the time to your local time.

The idea is that in the year of each person's birth, the Earth, sun, moon and surrounding planets exerted their combined influence in such a way that it left an imprint on each person's Chi. Once you understand the way your own Chi energy moves, it is then possible to predict how it will mix with the predominant Chi energy of any year. For example, someone who was born after 14:24 (GMT) on 3 February 1962, has a Nine Ki year number of 2. After 20:10 (GMT) on 3 February 1996 the number at the centre for that year is 4. By analyzing how the energy of someone with the Nine Ki year number 2 mixes with the Chi energy present in a Nine Ki year when 4 is in the middle, it is possible to predict how they will fare that year. Most importantly this will provide essential information to advise them on how they can make the most of that year.

The eight directions

In the Nine Ki charts, each number has a direction: each direction has a trigram associated with it. A trigram is three lines, which can be solid or broken. The solid lines are more yang and the broken lines more yin. The trigrams are taken from an ancient Chinese text: the I *Ching*. The Nine Ki number 5 does not have a trigram or direction as it is situated in the centre, so 5 is considered the most powerful of the numbers.

Each trigram has:
- a direction that describes the Chi energy in that direction
- one of the five elements associated with it. Where more than one direction share an element they also have a symbol
- a Nine Ki number, a colour that reflects the nature of the Chi energy and a time of day when the Chi energy in this part of the home is strongest.
- a member of the family that further describes the Chi energy.

   The references to the family are based on a traditional family, whose roles may seem out of date compared to a modern society.

One way to understand the nature of the trigrams is to describe each number using the analogy of the cycle of life. At the same time you should remember your own Nine Ki year number and see if the description for your number applies to a part of your character.

One north

Five Element	Family Member	Colour	Time
Water	Middle son	Off White	Night

The north of a home has a quiet energy that is associated with sex, spirituality and isolation. Although this energy seems passive on the surface, it carries great power. The image of the middle son is affectionate, but independent. North energy helps people to make deep changes within themselves.

In the cycle of life north represents conception. This is the phase of internal development, where energy is kept inside. It represents deep internal processes and thoughts. On the surface all appears quiet, but inside powerful changes are taking place.

The energy in the north of a building is suited to activities such as sleep, sex, meditation and creative activities. Suitable rooms are a bedroom, meditation room or artist's studio. The colour associated with water is off white or clear and shiny like varnish. This shade has an almost translucent quality and conveys an impression of depth and movement. Water Chi energy can change direction easily without disturbing the surrounding Chi energy too much.

Eight north-east

Five Element	Family Member	Colour	Time
Soil/Mountain	Youngest Son	White	Early Morning

The north-east of a building carries a strong, piercing energy. The youngest son has the image of a spoilt, competitive child. The Chi energy here is motivating, sharp and direct. In addition, the Chi energy of the north-east is very quick to change direction.
In the cycle of life the child has been born and is learning to interact with his or her environment. The child becomes self-motivated, and develops a strong sense of self.

The Chi energy of the north-east supports activities like exercise, games and play. This could include an exercise room, a games room and a children's playroom. White represents the Chi energy of the north east. This is a brilliant white, rather like snow-peaked mountains. This shade of white should create a shiny, sharp, hard atmosphere.

Three east

Five Element	Family Member	Colour	Time
Tree/Thunder	Eldest Son	Bright Green	Morning

The eastern segment of a building encourages an active, focused Chi energy. The eldest son represents the family's future. The energy of the east is associated with ambition, getting things started and putting ideas into practice. This type of Chi energy is good for a quick start. In the cycle of life, the child has grown to a young man or woman and is ready to begin his or her career. This is a time of great ambition and new beginnings.

The east is particularly suited to things that are active, practical and orientated towards building for the future. Rooms that would be supported by this kind of Chi energy include an office, kitchen or hobby room. A bedroom in the east would be helpful if the occupants wish their lives to be busier, are starting a new business or building up their careers.

Bright green is the closest colour to this type of Chi energy. The shade is lively and vibrant, stimulating feelings of growth, freshness and vitality. This is the green of new leaves.

Four south-east

Five Element	Family Member	Colour	Time
Tree/Wind	Eldest Daughter	Dark Green or Blue	Mid Morning

The south-east part of a building has busy, active Chi energy, but it is less focused and sharp than the Chi energy in the east. The eldest daughter is much gentler than the eldest son. This Chi encourages orderly and harmonious development. At this phase in the lifecycle a person is more mature and making more harmonious progress in their life.

Activities requiring an atmosphere that encourages communication, creativity and persistence will work well in the south-east. Rooms could include a kitchen, office or studio. A bedroom in the south-east will help the occupants develop their careers, but in a more gentle manner.

Dark green is closest to the Chi energy of the south-east. A more established, darker green than the vibrant, bright green of the east. Dark green represents leaves that are mature, but still instils feelings of growth and vitality. Blue can also be associated with this energy.

Nine south

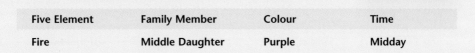

Five Element	Family Member	Colour	Time
Fire	Middle Daughter	Purple	Midday

The south is associated with fire, passion and brilliance. The character of the middle daughter is outgoing, extrovert and sociable. If the Chi in the south moves well, the occupants can expect fame and popularity. In the cycle of life this phase represents middle age, when our man or woman has reached a time to enjoy success.

The south is suited to sociable, outgoing, activities. A room for parties and entertaining would be ideal. In addition, the south is helpful for stimulating intelligence, so a room here can make a good study. Similarly, a bedroom here could benefit a student. However, the energy of the south is passionate and intense, so it may be difficult to concentrate or sleep well. This area is highly energetic, although less focused than in the east and south east.

Bright, fiery purple best represents the Chi energy of the south. It is the shade found at the root of a flame, and should instil feelings of passion, excitement and heat.

Two south-west

Five Element	Family Member	Colour	Time
Soil/Earth	Mother	Black	Afternoon

South-west Chi energy will be more settled and slow. The atmosphere is more conducive to consolidation and methodical progress. This creates a more cautious environment. The mother can encourage family harmony. In the cycle of life the man or woman has reached a more settled phase when they are more orientated towards family harmony. By now they may have grandchildren and wish to spend more time with their family.

The south-west is most suited to settled, homely activities. A family room, crafts or television room would work well here. In a building the segment to the south-west will help the occupants to make the most of and improve the quality of whatever they have.

Black is the colour that is most associated with the Chi energy of the south-west. The shade of black is similar to that found in very rich black soil or charcoal.

Seven west

Five Element	Family Member	Colour	Time
Metal/Lake	Youngest Daughter	Red	Early Evening

The west segment of a building has Chi energy associated with the harvest. This makes it an important area in terms of income. Red sunsets make this a potentially romantic place in the home. The youngest daughter gives this area a more playful quality that is associated with the pursuit of pleasure. In the cycle of life our man or woman has reached retirement age. It is time to relax and enjoy the fruits of their hard work

The energy of the west is ideally suited to the pursuit of pleasure, romance or money. Ideal rooms could include a dining room, or a room to entertain or relax in. A bedroom in the west could help you feel more romantic, fun-loving and able to focus on finance.

Red or pink are the colours of the Chi energy of the west. The shade is similar to a beautiful red sunset. It should bring out feelings of romance, joy and contentment.

Six north-west

Five Element	Family Member	Colour	Time
Metal/Heaven	Father	Silver Lining	Late Evening

The Chi energy of the north-west is associated with leadership, organization and planning ahead. The father adds authority, respect and responsibility. At this stage in the cycle of life the man or woman has been through the whole cycle and is in a position to help others through the earlier phases. For this reason the north-west part of a building is associated with planning ahead and organization, as well as leadership and wisdom.

Chi in the north-west of a building is ideal for activities that require organization and planning. An office, study, library or bedroom would all suit this type of atmosphere. A bedroom here would be most suited to the parents. In a commercial building the north-west is the ideal location for the chairman.

Silvery white is the colour that is closest to the kind of energy in the north-west.

Five centre

Five Element	Family Member	Colour	Time
Soil	None	Yellow	None

The Chi energy of the centre carries the greatest power. It is changeable and has two great extremes of power: productive and destructive. The nature of this Chi energy is such that it needs more open space. A hall and landing are ideal in the centre of a building.

   The colour of this central Chi energy is yellow. Yellow has the ability to mix well with all the other colours. Ideally it would bring out a feeling of being in the centre of things.

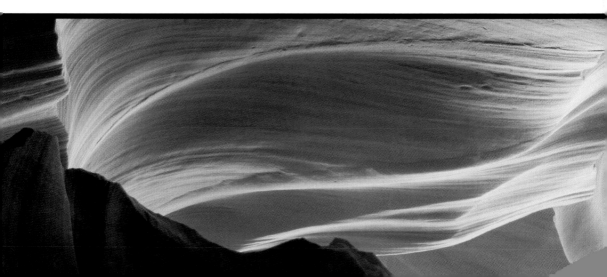

Applying Feng Shui

Using the compass to align the eight directions

To find out how Chi energy moves through your home, the grid with eight directions needs to be laid over a floor plan of your living or working space. You will need a compass, protractor, ruler, pencil and paper and tracing paper. The compass should be the kind that has an outer dial that can be rotated to take compass bearings.

First make a floor plan to scale of the space you wish to assess. If you have more than one floor, draw separate plans for each floor. If you live in an apartment just draw that apartment.

Next add the doors and windows. If you are not measuring their size and position try to draw them in proportion to the room.

The next task is to find the centre of your building. The easiest shapes are a rectangle, square, circle or octagon. The centre can be found simply by drawing diagonal lines between opposing corners or opposite points on a circle. These are all considered favourable shapes in Feng Shui.

More complicated is an L-shape. The simplest method is to break it down to two or more rectangles. Draw a line between the centres of each rectangle. Next break it down into two alternative rectangles and then draw a line between these two rectangles. The point at which the two lines between the centres cross is the centre of the whole area.

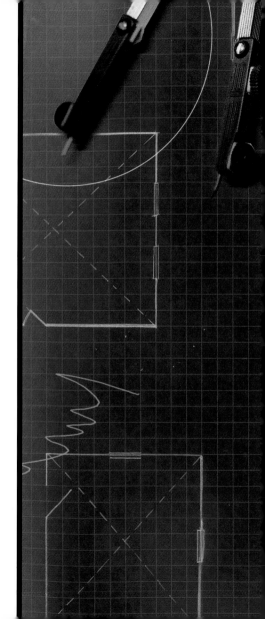

For a more complicated shape, look up how to find the centre in a geometry book, or draw the shape of the floor plan to scale on a piece of card. Cut out the card and use a needle to find the centre of gravity. Once the card balances on the needle, pierce the card. The hole will mark the centre of the building.

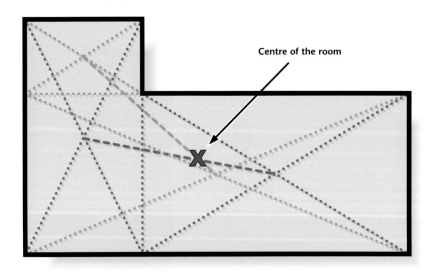

Finding the centre of an L-shaped room

Now find magnetic north. Take a compass and point it directly at one of the walls. Walk around, keeping your compass pointing towards the same wall. The needle may change direction as you do this. Things made of iron or steel will alter the magnetic field and electrical appliances will create their own field. Steel beams, pipes or water tanks may be concealed and can distort your readings. Once you have a consistent reading, hold the compass facing the wall and turn the outside dial until 0 lines up with the point of your needle. This is north. The marker line on your compass will now be lined up with a number on the dial. This number is the bearing that will be used to draw magnetic north on the floor plan.

To mark magnetic north on the floor plan, place the centre of a protractor over the centre of your floor plan. Turn the protractor until the same number that you took from the compass is facing the wall you used to take your compass reading. The number 0 on your protractor will now be facing the same direction on your floor plan as the needle of your compass in your building. Make a mark next to the 0 on your protractor, and draw a line from the centre of your floor through this mark. This line will be pointing towards magnetic north on your plan.

Copy the grid opposite onto tracing paper, or photocopy it onto a transparency, and lay it over your floor plan, making sure to line up the line pointing north on the plan to the line pointing north on your grid.

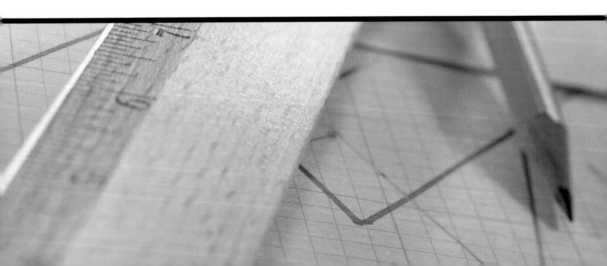

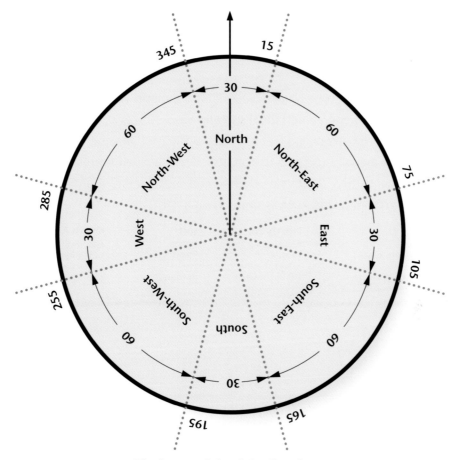

The layout of the eight directions

The shape of a building

The first aspect of your home to assess is its shape. A rectangle is most common and is considered ideal in Feng Shui. However, a long, narrow building will mostly occupy a few areas of the grid, leaving others empty. The areas of the grid that are filled will be well represented in the occupants' lives, whereas others could be deficient. A square will fill the grid evenly and is considered beneficial.

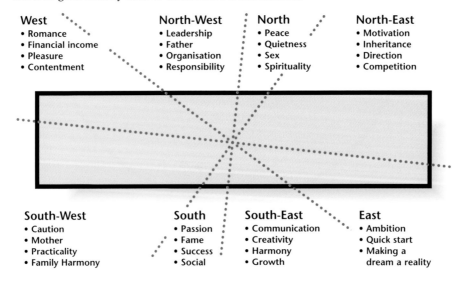

West
- Romance
- Financial income
- Pleasure
- Contentment

North-West
- Leadership
- Father
- Organisation
- Responsibility

North
- Peace
- Quietness
- Sex
- Spirituality

North-East
- Motivation
- Inheritance
- Direction
- Competition

South-West
- Caution
- Mother
- Practicality
- Family Harmony

South
- Passion
- Fame
- Success
- Social

South-East
- Communication
- Creativity
- Harmony
- Growth

East
- Ambition
- Quick start
- Making a dream a reality

Many buildings are irregular shapes. They either have parts missing or extensions. A missing part is an indentation that is less than half the length of the building, and an extension is where part of the building sticks out. To qualify as an extension it has to be less than half the length of the building. A small extension will enhance the Chi in that part of the building. A large extension can exaggerate the Chi too much, making the energy unbalanced. Listed below are the main influences of extensions or missing areas in particular directions of a building.

North

A moderate extension in the north could enhance spirituality. It may make the occupants' lives more peaceful and bring independence. It can be beneficial for fertility. A large extension may lead to the occupants becoming too isolated. They could become involved in a sexual scandal, feel lonely or find their lives are too quiet.

A missing space in the north would reduce the occupants' sexual vitality and fertility. It could also lead to a loss of income, increase feelings of stress and make it harder to maintain good health.

North-east

A small extension in the north-east would stimulate motivation, sense of direction and hard work. However, no extension would be preferable.

A large extension can cause the Chi energy to overwhelm the building. This can make the movement of energy through the home unstable. A large extension can lead to greed and allow the occupants to become too competitive with each other. This could increase the risk of jealousies.

A small missing space in the north-east can be advantageous, although none is preferable. A large missing space could lead to the occupants losing the desire to work, reduced motivation or a lack of direction.

East

A small extension to the east can be favourable in terms of careers and business. The occupants will be busy, energetic and active. This is suited to younger people who are actively building up their lives. This direction is

particularly favourable for starting new projects. A large extension may make the occupants too hectic or unable to relax. They may be tempted to rush to succeed and fail.

A missing space to the east may cause children to be less active or lose their ambition. It could make it harder to focus on your career and feel enthusiastic about new opportunities.

South-east

A minor extension in the south-east can bring harmony and encourage activity, helping careers and business. It would be generally favourable in terms of relationships and marriage. Generally, this shape is beneficial for prosperity. Too large an extension here can lead to over-activity and impatience.

A missing space in the south-east can result in disharmony and weakness in career or business. The occupants may become lazy. This could affect the occupants' ability to communicate their ideas. A large missing space in the south-east can cause stagnation.

South

A modest extension to the south may encourage fame, public recognition and success. In addition, the occupants may find they are more passionate and outgoing, particularly if involved in public affairs.

A large extension can lead to unrealistically high expectations, resulting in disappointment, or excessive passions leading to arguments and separation. Some might find it hard to stay at home in such a building.

A missing area to the south may make the occupants more vulnerable to law suits and public prosecution. They could be more susceptible to loneliness, isolation and feeling withdrawn.

South-west

A small extension in the south-west can encourage harmony and make the occupants more practical and methodical. Too big an extension can make the mother too dominant. In addition, the occupants could become over-cautious and find it harder to make decisions. The father might lose his enthusiasm for work.

A missing area in the south-west can weaken the mother. This could make it harder to achieve family harmony. The occupants feel less stable and prone to rash decisions.

West

A moderate extension in the west can increase income and be helpful for occupants seeking loans. It could also be beneficial for marriage. This shape can be supportive for entertaining. A large extension to the west may lead to loss of money, along with too great a preoccupation

with the pursuit of pleasure. Although this would affect everyone, younger females are likely to be influenced most.

A missing space in the west may lead to a lack of contentment. This would particularly affect the youngest daughter. A woman living in a building with this shape could find it harder to find a partner. The occupants might find it harder to be playful. A large missing area can lead to a loss of assets.

North-west

A modest extension in the north-west can be beneficial for careers. It is advantageous for planning ahead, having a clear head and developing a sense of justice. This shape will be supportive to the father or breadwinner. Too big an extension may result in the father, or main earner, becoming too powerful. This could lead to arrogance.

A missing area in the north-west can weaken the energy of the father or main wage earner. He could feel he has lost control.

The features of a building

Doors

Any entrance influences the flow of Chi, and a door that is used frequently will have a bigger influence than one that is used only occasionally. A door that opens into an open space will allow Chi energy to flow freely, but if a door opens into a narrow corridor the Chi can become congested.

To determine the effect of a door, look at the floor plan and decide in which of the eight directions the door is located. The door will tend to encourage the flow of that particular Chi energy into the building. Also look at the direction the door faces. The door may be to the east of the building, but face south. The direction of the door has a smaller influence than the position, but the principle is the same.

North

Generally, the energy of the north is too cold for a door or entrance. This Chi can make the occupants' lives quieter. A door in the north is good for hiding. People living or working here could find themselves becoming isolated. It could also increase feelings of insecurity or worry.

North-east

A north-east door can help create a refreshing atmosphere, encouraging the occupants to have a clear sense of direction. It can cause the movement of Chi energy to change suddenly, which may make the fortunes of the occupants susceptible to instability. Chi from the north-east is cold and piercing and would make the building less comfortable.

East

A door located to the east can be particularly helpful for young people. The east is a position that helps create a bright future. This influence is supportive to the occupants' careers and business. It is the direction that is most likely to lead to quick progress. Because a door to the east is beneficial for business, getting something new started and a bright future, it is a very good position for the entrance to a commercial building, particularly a new business.

South-east

A door located in the south-east will bring in Chi that encourages the occupants' lives to develop harmoniously. Chi energy from the south-east will help the occupants to be more creative and can lead the occupants to have good connections socially and in their business.

A door in the south-east can also help the occupants develop their careers or businesses.

South

A door in the south will allow more of the kind of Chi energy that creates fame and public recognition to enter. Chi energy from the south is advantageous for students and could lead the occupants of a house to be more sociable. A door in the south brings in a fiery, hot energy. This intense energy can make the occupants' lives more stressful and argumentative.

South-west

A door in the south-west is favourable for feeling settled. it brings an energy that can help improve the quality of relationships, family life and work. It is ideal for consolidation. The Chi energy of the south-west is not fast and can lead to slow progress in terms of the occupants' careers or business.

West

A door to the west is beneficial for romance and pleasure and focusing on the end result. The quality of Chi energy is settled. By bringing more of this west Chi energy into the building, the occupants can feel more content. This feeling of contentment may also, however, lead to the occupants feeling less motivated. A door in the west may help financial income, although it could also lead to excessive expenditure.

North-west

A door in the north-west will bring respect and dignity. A door here can make it easier for the occupants to win trust. North-western Chi energy brings in the qualities associated with leadership, organization and responsibility. These characteristics favour the parents of the family.

Water

Traditionally, the site of a well was considered of great importance to the family's health, prosperity and spiritual well-being. Nowadays, water would include the main water pipe to a building, a bathroom, a toilet, the kitchen sink, a pond, a swimming pool, a fountain, an aquarium and other indoor water features. Large water features nearby should also be taken into consideration. This includes rivers, lakes and the sea.

North

Any water to the north will be in its own element of water and would have a neutral effect. However, the Chi energy of the north tends to be cold and still. This can make it hard to get rid of dampness, moisture or humidity, so the north of a building would not be a good position for a bathroom. Constant dampness in the north could lead to frequent illnesses.

North-east

The north-east is the least desirable direction in which to have water. Water Chi energy does not mix well with the Chi of the north-east, which is soil. Of all features, a bathroom or toilet would be most harmful, because sudden movements of water, such as flushing a toilet, add to the unstable movements of Chi characteristic of this direction.

East

The element of water supports the tree Chi energy to the east. Generally, water in the east is considered favourable. As water here builds up the east Chi energy, the occupants could benefit in terms of their careers, activity and the ability to make their dreams a reality. A toilet to the east is less harmful than to the south, south-west, west, north or north-east. However, a toilet that has no windows is always a problem, wherever it is located.

South-east

Chi energy to the south-east is also associated with tree Chi. Again, water Chi energy will support the tree Chi energy of the south-east. In this direction water helps the occupants in terms of communication, creativity and the ability to develop their lives harmoniously.

South

The Chi energy of water is the opposite to the southern Chi energy of fire. So water features are generally considered harmful when located to the south. The occupants of such a building could be more prone to law suits, loss of reputation and suppressed emotions. They might find it hard to express themselves.

South-west

The Chi energy in the south-west is associated with soil. Soil Chi has the ability to destroy water Chi so it is not recommended to have a water feature to the south-west. In oriental medicine, water Chi energy is considered to be the source of all Chi energy. When water is located south-west, the Chi energy that the water brings in is destroyed by the soil and the occupants can be more prone to illnesses.

West

The Chi energy to the west is considered to be metal. Water in the west can create the effect of drawing the metal Chi energy of the west. This is most likely if a bathroom or toilet are situated to the west. In this case, the occupants of the building are susceptible to financial losses and difficulties in finding romance.

North-west

Water in the north-west will have a similar effect as in the west, although water coming into the building from this direction could work harmoniously with the Chi energy of the north-west. I would not recommend a toilet or bathroom here. This could lead to a weakness in terms of organization, responsibility and planning ahead.

Exactly the same process of examining the influence of a feature and assessing how this will affect the Chi energy of each of the eight directions can be applied to other features within your building. Other features that you should consider include fireplaces (fire Chi energy), safes for money (metal Chi energy) and any tall plants (tree Chi energy). Stairs and windows will have a very similar influence to the door.

The direction
and timing of a move

One of the biggest influences on health and prosperity is the timing
and direction of a move, for this determines how our own Chi energy
mixes with the new energy in which we find ourselves. In order to
calculate: a) the best time to move in a certain direction; b) the effects
of moves you made in the past, and c) when to change the flow of Chi
energy in a part of a building, you will need your Nine Ki year number
and the Nine Ki chart for the year in which you want to move. These
can be found on page 27–8. The method is the same as for laying the
eight directions over a building. Mark your home on a map with an X.
Draw a line from your home going due north. Then draw on the eight
directions or place a transparency so that the centre is over your home
and north on the transparency is aligned with north on your map. Note
the direction of your proposed move.

Harmful Moves

The following are six types of moves that can be harmful. They are in order
of importance: the first four can potentially cause the greatest harm.

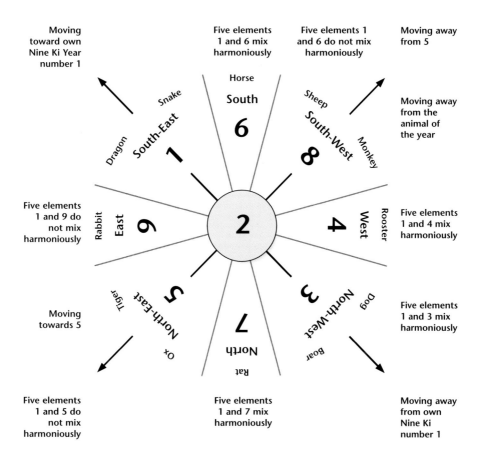

Moving toward own Nine Ki Year number 1

Five elements 1 and 6 mix harmoniously

Five elements 1 and 6 do not mix harmoniously

Moving away from 5

Moving away from the animal of the year

Five elements 1 and 4 mix harmoniously

Five elements 1 and 3 mix harmoniously

Moving away from own Nine Ki number 1

Five elements 1 and 7 mix harmoniously

Five elements 1 and 5 do not mix harmoniously

Moving towards 5

Five elements 1 and 9 do not mix harmoniously

Snake
South-East
Dragon
1

Horse
South
6

Sheep
South-West
Monkey
8

Rabbit
East
9

2

Rooster
West
4

Tiger
North-East
Ox
5

Rat
North
7

Boar
North-West
Dog
3

An example of someone with the Nine Ki Year number 1 moving in a year when 2 is in the centre and it is the year of the tiger

Towards the position of 5

When you move towards 5, you are moving in the direction of great power. As this power can work destructively, the risk is too great. Small problems can rapidly develop into serious ones. For example, in a year when 2 is in the centre of the chart, 5 is in the north-east. Anyone moving north-east, regardless of their Nine Ki year number, will be moving towards 5. If your own Nine Ki number is 5, this means you are moving towards both 5 and your own Nine Ki year number.

Moving away from 5

Moving away from 5 is travelling away from the power centre. In a year when 2 is in the centre of the chart, anyone will move away from 5 if they move south-west. If your own Nine Ki year number is 5, moving away from 5 means you are moving away from both 5 and your own number. This makes the move potentially more harmful.

Moving away from 5 risks feeling tired, losing your focus and being prone to accidents.

Moving towards your own Nine Ki year number

Try to avoid moving towards your own Nine Ki number. For example, if someone with the Nine Ki year number 1 moves south-east when 2 is in the centre of the chart, they are moving towards their own number.

Essentially, this is like trying to push two magnets together when both poles have the same charge. Forcing your own Chi energy in a direction that has the same energy that year can lead to poor health, stress and a confused mental state.

Moving away from your own Nine Ki year number

Moving away from your own number is also considered harmful. In a year when 2 is in the centre of the chart, a person who has the Nine Ki year number 1 will be moving away from their own Chi energy when they move north-west. Moving away from a direction that has the same energy is like leaving part of yourself behind. People describe it as a loss of confidence. It can lead to feelings of disorientation and an inability to organize your life properly.

Moving away from the animal of the year

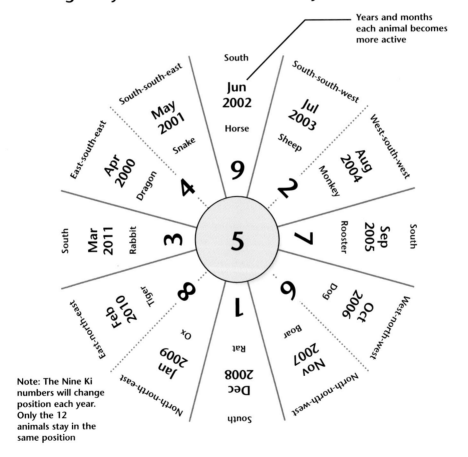

Years and months each animal becomes more active

South

South-south-east

South-south-west

East-south-east

West-south-west

May 2001

Jun 2002

Jul 2003

Snake

Horse

Sheep

Apr 2000

Aug 2004

Dragon

Monkey

9

2

South

South

Mar 2011

Rabbit

Rooster

Sep 2005

3

5

7

Tiger

Dog

Feb 2010

Oct 2006

8

1

6

East-north-east

West-north-west

Ox

Rat

Boar

Jan 2009

Dec 2008

Nov 2007

North-north-east

South

North-north-west

4

Note: The Nine Ki numbers will change position each year. Only the 12 animals stay in the same position

To calculate this you need to include the 12 Chinese animals. The diagram opposite shows the standard Nine Ki chart with 5 in the centre and the 12 animals in their positions around the chart. The animals always stay in these positions regardless of the year. However, each year one of the animals becomes more active so there is an additional concentration of energy in the corresponding direction. At the end of each year the next animal in a clockwise direction becomes the animal to represent that year.

Moving away from the animal of the year is considered to lead to a deficiency of energy and, in particular, to situations breaking up. This could be the break-up of a relationship, separation from a family or the break-down of business negotiations or contracts.

Moving away from the animal of the month

The diagram opposite also shows the month that is associated with each animal. These never change, so December is always the month of the Rat, January always the month of the Ox and so on. Chinese months normally start between the 3rd and 9th of our month, depending on the month and year. The charts for these dates can be found in books on Nine Ki or Oriental astrology.

The principle is the same as for moving away from the animal of the year, except the influence of such a move is smaller and more temporary.

Finally, to move in a direction that will help improve your life it is important to move towards a number whose Five Element Chi energy is in harmony with your own Five Element Chi energy.

For example, someone with the Nine Ki year chart of 1 has the Chi energy associated with water. When 2 is in the centre position, 7 is in the north. The number 7 has the Five Element Chi energy of metal. Metal and water Chi energy mix harmoniously with each other. I would therefore expect this move to be positive.

Read the description of each of the eight directions on pages 31–9 to discover what kind of influence each direction will have. To consider all the factors involved in determining the best time and direction for a

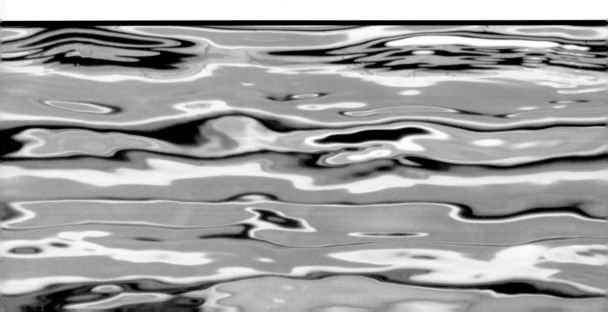

move requires lots of experience and practice so, if you wish to be totally sure, seek professional advice.

The following are some basic guidelines for a permanent move from one home to another:

• The direction you move is from the place you have been sleeping for at least three months to the next destination. It is not the route you choose to get there.
• To establish yourself in the new Chi energy, you need to sleep every night in the new location for at least two months, preferably three.
• The bigger the distance you move, the stronger and quicker the effects.

The same principles should be used when considering making changes to a building.

Feng Shui Solutions

There are two ways to help enhance your life with Feng Shui. The first is to place yourself so that your own Chi energy is positively influenced by the flow of Chi energy through a building. The second is to change the way Chi energy moves through a building.

Positioning yourself

Beds

There are three considerations. First, which room to sleep in, secondly, where to place the bed and thirdly, which direction the bed should face. The position within the home will have a bigger influence than the position within the bedroom. However, the direction the bed faces has a significant influence. When I refer to the direction a bed faces I mean the direction the top of the occupant's head points towards.

Each of the eight directions generates Chi energy that will charge your own Chi as you sleep.

North

Sleeping in the north or facing north is ideal for quiet sleep. It calms Chi energy and enhances spirituality. North is not recommended for young people or anyone who is trying to advance their career. Neither would I recommend it for someone who is lonely. The north may encourage sexual activity.

North-east

Sleeping in the north-east or facing north-east provides motivating, competitive and sharp Chi energy. Generally, the north-east is not recommended for sleep. It can cause nightmares and restlessness. Placing the children in the north-east can make the parents' whole lives revolve around their children.

East

Sleeping in the east or facing east can be ideal for building up your career. This is a particularly favourable direction for young people. East can be beneficial for becoming more active, more ambitious and having the ability to put your dreams into practice.

South-east

By facing the south-east you could see positive developments in your career. The Chi energy of the south-east also has a creative, imaginative nature and can help communication.

South

The Chi energy of the south is ideal for passion, intelligence and fame. Occupants sleeping here might find themselves lying awake thinking. In spite of this, sleeping in the south or facing south could help a young student, actor or sales person.

South-west

The Chi of the south-west can influence the occupants to become more settled, practical and realistic. It is ideal for finding ways to improve your quality of life and making the most of what you already have.

West

If you seek more pleasure and romance in life, try sleeping in the west or facing west. It can help you focus on the end result and complete projects. It may lead to greater contentment with life.

North-west

Sleeping in the north-west or facing north-west is the classic position for leadership. This is the ideal place for parents or people who have reached a stable phase in life. North-west Chi energy can lead to greater responsibility and the ability to organize and plan ahead.

Desk and chairs

The art of choosing a place to work or sit involves, first, being clear about what you want to achieve and secondly, deciding which kind of Chi energy will be most helpful to you. Apart from the position and direction, you should try, if possible, to sit so that you face the rest of the room and the door to the room.

Here are examples of places I often recommend to work in.

In the east facing east

This is ideal if you are starting a new career or business, in the early stages of your working life, or for a young person. The Chi energy of the east helps stimulate a quick start, makes you more active and increases the ability to make your dream a reality.

In the north-west facing south-east

This is the classic position for the leader or chairman of a company. The Chi energy here helps to develop organizational skills, along with the ability to plan ahead and generate feelings of responsibility. In addition, this direction is associated with respect, authority and trust. All are essential qualities for someone in a leadership position.

The same principles apply to finding the best location to sit to relax, to eat or for meetings. For example, sitting in the west part of a home in the evening would be relaxing and help you feel more content.

It is not always possible to find the ideal place for a bed, desk or chairs, therefore part of the skill of a Feng Shui consultant is to create solutions in a limited space. Remember that it is important to make sure the timing of these changes is favourable.

Altering the flow of chi energy

There are many ways of altering the flow of Chi.

Water

Water Chi energy supports the tree Chi energy of the east and south-east. Therefore, water placed in either of these directions will build up the energy associated with the occupant's career. In the east, water would be more useful for making a quick start, for ambition and putting ideas into practice, whereas in the south-east, water would be better for communication, creativity and developing life harmoniously. Water features include fountains, ponds, swimming pools, rivers, lakes, an ocean, aquaria and indoor water fountains. It is important that the water is fresh and clean. Stagnant or dirty water could have a negative effect.

Sea salt

Placing a small bowl of sea salt next to a door to the north-east stabilizes the quickly changing soil Chi energy of the north-east. This will make the occupant's life more stable and less vulnerable to outside influences. You should also put salt in the south-west. Salt in the north-east and south-west is helpful even if there are no doors there.

Iron

This includes items made of cast iron and metals that contain iron. Iron is associated with metal Chi energy, and stabilizes the flow of Chi. Iron alters the flow of the local magnetic field, and should be used with care. Iron is not as effective at stabilizing Chi energy as salt. A black cast-iron pot could be very effective in the south-west part of a building if you wish to make the Chi energy there more calm and solid.

Plants

In general, growing plenty of plants in a building will create a more fresh, alive atmosphere. Plants with pointed leaves will tend to help move Chi more quickly and are useful in internal corners. Plants with round, floppy leaves tend to calm the flow of Chi energy and are effective in front of an external or protruding corner. Bushy plants help slow fast-moving Chi energy and can work well in long corridors or near doors.

Mirrors

As Chi energy behaves in a similar way to light, mirrors can be used to change the direction of the flow of Chi energy. Mirrors staggered on either side of a long corridor will move the Chi from side to side, slowing its flow along the corridor. Large mirrors can also be used to give the impression that a room extends into a missing area. They should be large enough, and positioned so that the reflection does not cut off the top of any of the occupants' heads.

Feng Shui consultants use a small, round, convex mirror. This has the effect of reflecting and spreading Chi energy. This would be useful, for example, when trying to stop Chi energy flowing towards a door. If you have mirrors in your bedroom, position them so that they do not point towards your bed, or cover them with a cloth.

Lighting

Lights can be used to brighten a stagnant corner and stimulate the movement of potentially stagnant Chi. Lights that shine upwards are particularly useful. They are helpful when directed onto a sloping ceiling or in a building with low ceilings. When deciding where to place lights, think of the areas where you wish to keep an active flow of Chi. Fluorescent lighting is not good for health or concentration.

Crystals

Hanging a crystal in a sunlit window will produce a pattern of light on the walls of a room. This is helpful when you wish to move more Chi

energy into a stagnant room. Hang crystals in the window of a room
that has dark corners or feels dull.

Wind chimes

The ringing of a wind chime or bell stimulates Chi energy and has a
cleansing effect. Choose a wind chime that makes a sound that
resonates. The wind chime needs to ring in order to be effective. Any
sound in a building will influence the movement of Chi energy, so it is
worth considering all the various items that make sound and choosing
versions that make harmonious sounds.

Coping with classic problems

The following are examples of classic Feng Shui problem areas.

A building at the top of a t-junction

As cars approach a T-junction, they direct the flow of Chi towards the building opposite. This places the occupants in the path of a funnel of fast-moving Chi. To slow the movement, grow a hedge and bushes in the front garden. As the Chi from the traffic passes through the hedge it begins to move more slowly. To deflect the Chi energy away, position a round, convex mirror on the wall facing the road.

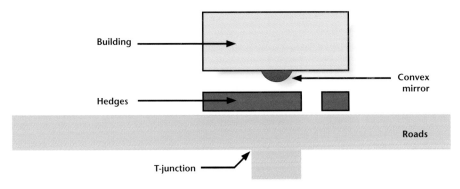

Building

Convex mirror

Hedges

Roads

T-junction

Cutting Chi

Any protruding corner will make the passing Chi energy swirl, which can be disorientating. It may occur inside a building, such as in an L-shaped room, or when the corner of another building points towards your building. To avoid this grow a plant in front of the corner. Outside, a bush or tree would be suitable. A convex mirror facing the protruding corner will reflect and spread out some of the cutting Chi.

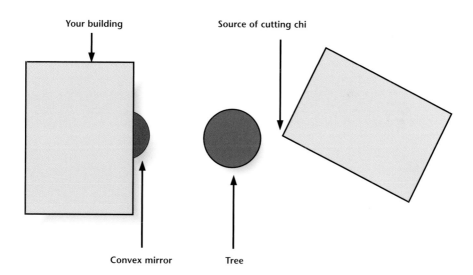

Your building

Source of cutting chi

Convex mirror

Tree

Long corridors

Chi energy tends to speed up and flow quickly along a corridor. To slow the Chi energy you can place indoor plants, staggered on either side of the corridor, or hang large mirrors at staggered points on either side of the corridor. Avoid shiny floors as they will make the Chi flow faster.

Stairs

Stairs carry the flow of Chi energy between floors. They often have a relatively high traffic flow of people, which makes them busy places in terms of Chi energy. Use sea salt, iron or stone to calm the flow of energy. Use the direction of the stairs to decide which would be more helpful. Stairs that lead straight to the front door, or any door that opens to the outside, are considered to direct Chi energy straight at the door. This can lead to a deficiency in energy within the building, which may lead to financial difficulties. A convex mirror can be used to reflect some of the Chi energy away from the door and a large, leafy plant between the stairs and door will help slow the movement of Chi. A wind chime hung between the stairs and door could also help spread the Chi energy out.

Front door in line with the back door

When you open the front door and are able to see the back door, Chi energy is free to move quickly between the doors. It is likely to enter the building and leave again without circulating. Growing plants between the doors can slow the movement between them, and mirrors can be used to deflect the Chi into other parts of the building. A wind chime will help spread the energy each time it rings.

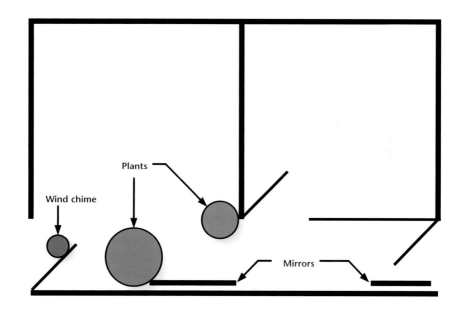

Wind chime

Plants

Mirrors

Narrow rooms

When you apply the eight directions to a narrow building or room, some directions take up large areas, whereas other directions have very little space. This makes it less likely that the occupants will benefit from a balance of Chi energy. Large mirrors can be used to create the impression that the room is twice as wide.

Clutter

Any kind of clutter in a building will slow the flow of Chi energy and increase the risk of stagnation. To refresh the Chi energy throughout a building, organize regular cleaning sessions in which all cupboards, storage areas and closets are emptied out and reorganized. Get rid of anything that is no longer of use to you. Clean, open spaces have the freshest Chi energy.

A Checklist for Buying your own Home

The following is a simple checklist you can apply to your existing home or workplace, or to a new building you intend moving into. It is not an exhaustive list but includes the most important aspects.

1 The Direction of Your Move
Check that the direction you and your family are moving in, in a particular year, is in harmony with the Chi energy of your and their Nine Ki year numbers.

2 The Well-being of the Previous Owners
Try to find out what happened to the previous owners. If they were

happily married, had successful careers and enjoyed good health, it is more likely that the home has favourable Chi energy.

3 Exposure to Sun
Good exposure to sunlight and natural light brings more Chi energy into a building and helps keep Chi energy moving. A bright, sunlit building is unlikely to suffer from stagnation.

4 The Position of Water
Find out if there is any water close to the building. If there is, check the direction in which it is located. East or south-east would be ideal.

5 The Position of the Main Gate and Door
Check the direction of the main entrance to the land and the main door to the building. Directions that are generally favourable are east, south-east, west and north-west.

6 The Effect of the Landscape

In Feng Shui it is recommended that the high ground is to the north, with the south side of a building open to sunlight. Check whether any roads point at the building. Being close to a busy road has a disturbing effect on the flow of Chi energy in a building. Avoid a building that is located in the shadow of another building. A river that runs away from a building can take Chi energy away from a building, leaving it deficient. Try to find out whether people are successful in that area and what they are successful for. Some Feng Shui schools advise against moving into a building from which you can see another building where people are dying. This includes hospitals, churches, funeral parlours, crematoriums and graveyards. One problem traditional Feng Shui practitioners did not have to deal with was electrical radiation and toxic waste. Locate any high voltage electrical power lines, transformers, electrical substations, electric railway lines and microwave transmitters. A home should be at least 800 metres away from any significant electrical radiation. A site within 50 kilometres of a nuclear power plant or waste processing plant would not be good Feng Shui. A land survey will determine whether the site has been polluted by toxic waste. Healthy-looking vegetation is generally a good sign.

7 Siting of Trees

Large trees to the south and east of a building will deprive the building of sunlight. Trees to the north and north-west are advantageous.

8 The Position of the Kitchen

The ideal position for a kitchen is to the east or south-east. The north-east is considered particularly unhelpful.

9 The Position of the Bathroom and Toilet

North, east or south-east are directions that are potentially less of a problem than north-east, south-west, west, north-west or south. A bathroom or toilet in the north-east is considered least desirable. Bathrooms and toilets that have windows are less of a problem.

10 Options for the Beds, Study and Layout of the Rooms

When looking throughout a building check that you will be able to position your beds, desk and chairs in favourable locations facing a helpful direction.

11 The Shape of the House

Look at the shape of the building. Rectangular, octagonal or round are the easiest shapes. If the building is an irregular shape, determine which areas are extensions or missing spaces, check their direction and look up how they affect the flow of Chi energy.

12 Stairs

Stairs that lead straight to the front door make a building less desirable. Stairs that cut through the centre of a building can disrupt the flow of Chi energy and are, therefore, considered unfavourable.

Guidelines for Practising Feng Shui

There is no such thing as the perfect Feng Shui building. Every building has something that disturbs the flow of Chi. The primary question is whether this has a negative influence. Your first objective is to discover whether the occupants are having problems. If they are not, then the disturbance is obviously not creating difficulties. Try not to create problems that do not exist. If the occupants are having problems, make sure you can match their problems with your assessment of their building. Once you have achieved this, the potential solutions will become clear.

When you start using Feng Shui I would advise you to keep it very simple. Start using yin and yang. Once you have become experienced at using yin and yang, move on to the five elements. Then, when you feel confident with the five elements, start using the eight directions.

Above all, keep your common sense! Often, the most effective Feng Shui solutions are very simple and subtle. Change the things in a building that are most practical, before attempting anything that requires major changes.

Finding Out More

Simon Brown works as a full-time Feng Shui consultant, lecturing on Feng Shui in both Britain and the United States. To find out about a Feng Shui consultation call 020 7431 9897, or write to Simon Brown, PO Box 10453, London, NW3 4WD, Tel: 020 7431 9897, Fax: 020 7431 9897, website: www.chienergy.co.uk or email him at simon@chienergy.co.uk.

Other Books by Simon Brown

- **Feng Shui Food**, Thorsons, ISBN: 0 7225 3934 7.
- **Practical Feng Shui**, Cassell & Co., ISBN: 0 7063 7634 X
- **Practical Feng Shui Astrology**, Ward Lock, ISBN: 0 7063 7825 3
- **Practical Feng Shui Solutions**, Cassell & Co., ISBN: 0 7304 35476 7
- **The Practical Art of Face Reading**, Carroll & Brown, ISBN: 1 903258 08 1
- **The Principles of Feng Shui**, Thorsons, ISBN: 0 7225 3347 0
  (This is also available as an audio cassette)
- **Practical Feng Shui for Business**, Ward Lock, ISBN: 0 7063 7768 0
- **Essential Feng Shui**, Cassell & Co., ISBN: 0 7063 7854 7